Los Alamos Rolodex

Doing Business with the National Lab

1967–1978

Introduction

A few years ago these business cards, embedded in a set of "rolodexes," emerged from the Black Hole of Los Alamos, which had by then reversed its polarity and was spewing, instead of sucking in.

The Black Hole was established and run, partially as a retail operation, for more than fifty years by Edward Grothus. Officially the Los Alamos Sales Company, it was started in the 1950s, when Grothus worked as a machinist and technician at the local Lab—that is, Los Alamos National Laboratory, the place where the atomic bomb was developed in secret in World War II, and which continued after the war as the nation's primary atomic weapons development center, joined later by Lawrence Livermore Lab in California.

Making atomic bombs from scratch requires a lot of technology, and in the process the Lab generated a lot of surplus, excess, and waste. As is the general rule at such places, surplus is directed to other government or educational entities or is auctioned off to the public. In the early years, as a worker at the Lab, Grothus was among the first to see what might be heading out the door, and he could be among the first in line to acquire it. As a professional hardware guy, he had an appreciation for interesting machines, milled materials, and exotic industrial artifacts. And Los Alamos Lab was exploring the outer limits of material science like nowhere else on earth.

Grothus quit the Lab in 1969, citing political differences between himself and atomic destruction. With a sense of humor and moral conviction, like a humanistic priest of reason, he became an outspoken antinuclear activist in a town that exists to make the bomb. He bought a small church in 1973 and dubbed it the First Church of High Technology. Dressed as a cardinal, he presided over "critical mass."

A few years later he bought the former grocery store next door and moved his surplus hardware inventory there. As at the Lab, where materials and resources flowed in and relatively little came out, the Los Alamos Sales Company's stock influx was much brisker than its decrease. Like most collectors, Grothus was retentive, and like the Lab, his business too became a bit of a black hole. Eventually he officially acknowledged that, placing a big BLACK HOLE sign over the front door and a smaller sign below: MUSEUM OF NUCLEAR WASTE.

Creative minded with an appreciation of the absurd, Grothus was astounded by the amount of perfectly functional, very rare, expensive equipment that was being cast aside by the Lab in its federally funded race toward the state of the art.

The shelves of the former grocery store were soon overflowing with electronic test equipment, sensors, optical components, centrifuges, curiously machined plastics, metals, and rack-mounted equipment. Hollywood set dressers used his material for props for movies (including the 1983 film *Silkwood*, the story of the whistleblower Karen Silkwood, another nuclear industry worker turned antinuclear activist). Prominent artists, including Larry Bell and Tony Price, discovered the Black Hole's bounty and mined it for use in their work. And award-winning filmmaker Ellen Spiro captured the spirit of the place in her 2002 documentary *Atomic Ed and the Black Hole*.

For many years, the Black Hole was a store where things were for sale, but it was also a museum of stunning complexity, and Grothus was the lone curator. He would animatedly explain the form and function anytime someone asked, "What's this thing?," a frequent question from visitors who browsed the racks and bins of the Black Hole. He was the nuclear lab's public techno archeologist and techno interpreter.

After more than thirty years of keeping the store stuffed to the limit, Ed Grothus died, in 2009. His children kept the business open without restocking it, perhaps hoping it would all just dwindle and go away, leaving the real estate finally out from under the pile, which would then be sold. So far, that has not happened.

Although the best stuff was long ago sold, given to museums, or stored elsewhere by his family, what remains of the Black Hole in its post–Ed Grothus spewing is mostly office dregs—metal desks, racks, shelving, chairs, adding machines, and even office trailers, full of more office stuff. Members of the Center for Land Use Interpretation often visited Ed Grothus and the Black Hole over the years, but it was amid this posthumous disgorging that we stumbled onto the rolodexes.

Divided into seven rotating desktop business card storage devices are thousands of cards. These rolodex-type card indexers were patented by the Dial-A-Card company, but like the names *Band-Aid* or *Kleenex*, the word *rolodex* is what became the generic descriptor for the whole genre.

The cards are arranged alphabetically over the lot of the seven rolodexes, but two letters, *A* and *C*, were missing. Like the industry the business cards relate to, the collection thus remains open ended, indefinite. Despite its sweeping span, this collection of cards represents an arbitrary, random grouping of contacts, kept by someone unknown in some unknown office; carefully amassed over fourteen years, it wound up in a pile of junk that nobody wanted, in a black hole.

Recorded on the back of each business card, inscribed by hand or stamped, is what is presumably the date that the card entered the collection. These range from the mid-1960s to 1978, a busy period in the development of nuclear weapons, during which almost half of the United States's nuclear tests were performed: around 450 out of the 1,030 total. In 1963, after treaties banned open-air testing of nuclear devices, the testing program went underground, literally. The work of these remarkably complex engineering projects, many costing tens of millions of dollars each, was shared by Lawrence Livermore and Los Alamos, competing nonprofits run by the University of California.

The collection of cards presents a record of companies that supplied goods and services to the nuclear industry, including everything from major military contractors to small, obscure high-tech widget suppliers—many of which are no longer extant (out of business or, more likely, bought and folded into larger military suppliers). Together, they are a historical snapshot of American high-tech corporations, their logos and graphics locked in time.

The synergies between the business community and America's global atomic and engineering might are brought to light in this indexical connection, directly linking the sources and methods of building and operating the most sophisticated and powerful national defense technologies in the world, in the not too distant past. Though the companies have morphed, the historic sinews embedded in the rolodexes explain much and suggest that much still remains to be explained.

As a historical record, they are relevant to an understanding of the present—they are hard evidence of the business relationships that built the transformative and secret technology that our nation still uses to dominate globally. Atomic bombs and their associated infrastructure were the heart of the "military-industrial complex," which, after the war, many believe became the political and economic core of the United States. These business cards are the synapses of this empire, each one the tip of an iceberg that may never be explored.

It takes a lot of technology to make technology, but ultimately the bomb was made by people calling other people on the phone. Although these cards are corporate, by definition, they are also personal. The cards name names: the individual salesmen who came calling, or were called upon, to do business with other lab contractors, who also, presumably, had their own business cards. The cards are even intimate, listing direct phone numbers, few of which seem to be in service anymore. Some of these people may even still be out there, at home or in retirement communities, though most will by now have moved on to greener pastures. In this way these cards today represent the opposite of what they originally were meant to do—connect people to people, seller to buyer. These cards are now dead ends. Obsolete, ephemeral minutiae. Expired information, spilling out of the wreckage of a former black hole, at the end of the atomic pile.

—Matthew Coolidge
The Center for Land Use Interpretation

1967

FRANK M. NOFSINGER
PLANT MANAGER

1701 N. GARDEN — P. O. BOX 97   505 623-5621
ROSWELL, NEW MEXI[illegible]8201   TWX 910-986-0074

Engineering and Manufacturing Vapor Control and Fire Prevention Equipment

THE PROTECTOSEAL COMPANY

1920 S. WESTERN AVENUE • CHICAGO, ILLINOIS 60608

WESTERN WAREHOUSE
4802 LOMA VISTA AVE.
LOS ANGELES, CALIF. 90058
PHONE: (213) 583-4183
TWX (213) 733-5400
WIRE XJK-FAX

CONRAD R SEIM
ENGINEERING REPRESENTATIVE

BOB HORTON
Field Support Engineer

PULVERIZING MACHINERY
DIVISION OF SLICK INDUSTRIAL COMPANY
Summit, New Jersey 07901
(201[illegible] 6360

M. A. NILES
BIAX MEMORY PRODUCTS

BIAX

FROM LOS ANGELES
625-7645

PHONE 546-7160
AREA CODE 714

1968

33 UNIVERSITY ROAD, CAMBRIDGE, MASSACHUSETTS 02138, Tel: 617 864-7420

MICHAEL D. PAGE
MANAGER, NEUTRON PRODUCTS
LABORATORY INSTRUMENT DIVISION
EXT. 225

B&F instruments. Inc.

Cornwells Heights
Pennsylvania, 19020

EUGENE FRANK
President

(215) MErcury 9-7100

ENGINEERING
FOR INDUSTRY
AND GOVERNMENT

BRAINPOWER U.S.A.

B. J. BRYAN
Vice-President/Regional Manager

phone **404**-422-7383
843 HUNTINGTON ROAD, SU[illegible] 2, MARIETTA, GEORGIA 30060

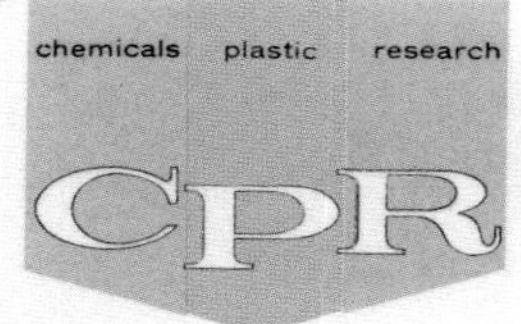

CPR DIVISION, THE UPJOHN COMPANY

555 Alaska Avenue • Torrance, California 90503

320-3550 775-6551 Area Code 213

H. GERSTIN

VICE PRESIDENT

DELTRONIC CORPORATION

K. R. (KEN) PARLEE
SALES ENGINEER

(714) 545-0401
929 BAKER STREET
COSTA MESA, CALIF. 92626

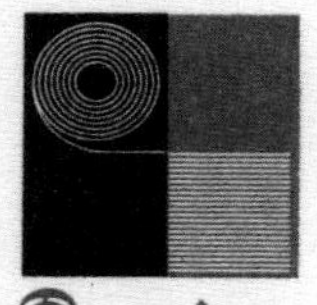

Dennison
COPIER

MICHAEL L. SMITH
REGIONAL DEALER MANAGER

DENNISON MANUFACTURING COMPANY
391 BEACH RD. - BURLINGA[illegible]ALIF. 94010 - TEL.: 347-2168

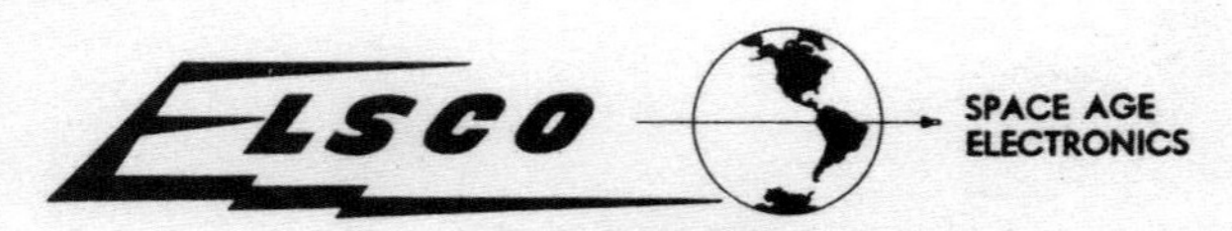

ELSCO NEW MEXICO, INC.

DAVID T. NICHOLLS
REGIONAL SALES MANAGER
RES. (505) 296-5127

412 SAN MATEO, N.E.
SUITE 1-D
ALBUQUERQUE, NEW MEXICO 87108
(505) 268-6016

Environments for Industry and Medicine

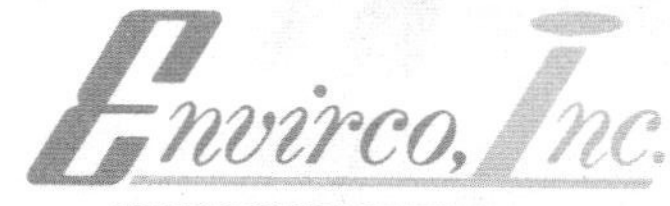

(FORMERLY COMFORT AIR SERVICE, INC.)

SUBSIDIARY OF BECTON, DICKINSON AND COMPANY

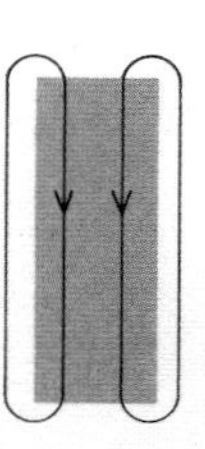

JIM WOODS

ENGINEER

TELEPHONE 243-7823, AREA 505

630 HAINES AVENU ALBUQUERQUE, NEW MEXICO 87107

ACADEMY 9-3405
AREA CODE 816

FIKE METAL PRODUCTS CORP.

L. L. (LES) FIKE

704 SOUTH 10TH STREET
BLUE SPRINGS, MISSOURI

BRUCE KINKNER

BRUCE KINKNER ASSOCIATES

746 WEST PALM LANE • [illegible]ENIX, ARIZONA • 272-7951

NUCLEAR SEMICONDUCTOR, INC.

LOUIS C. WANG
President

537 OLD COUNTY ROAD, SAN CARLOS, CALIFORNIA 94070 (415) 592-1633

W W "BILL" HALL

TERRITORY TECHNICAL REPRESENTATIVE

PAKO CORPORATION

6300 OLSON HIGHWAY (612) 540-6011
MINNEAPOLIS, MINNESOTA 55440

M[illegible]urers of Equipment for Photographic,
X-[illegible]aphic Arts and Motion Picture Industries

(415) 939-6602

ED BEARD
PRESIDENT

RADēCO

RADIATION DETECTING EQUIPMENT/INC.

P.O. Box 23162 Pleasant Hill, Calif. 94523

RESEARCH ▪ DEVELOP NT ▪ MANUFACTURING

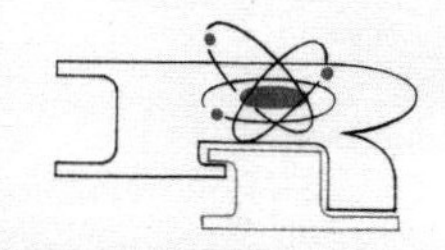

RESEARCH INSTRUMENT CO.

450 24TH. AVE. N.W. • NORMAN, OKLAHOMA 73070

PRODUCT DEVELOPMENT • PRECISION MACHINE SHOP

FRANK MAGINNIS
PROFESSIONAL ENGINEER

PHONE JE 4-7831

Phone 242-9882

Hot and Cold Typographic Service
For The Graphic Arts Trade

Sandia Composition Service

D. E. "Bud" NOLTENSMEYER

220 Gold Avenue, S.W.
Albuquerque, N. M.

SENSORMATIC OF
ALBUQUERQUE, INC.

DONALD L. CLEMAN

P. O. Box 1441
Roswell, New Mexico 88201
(505) 622-7445; 623-6915

Service:
Mesa Electric Co.
Albuquerque, New Mexico
(505) 255-1092; 255-3508

GARY F. SIPPLE, Sales Engineer

1140 W. Evelyn Ave., Sunny[illegible] Calif. 94086 (408) 245-1000

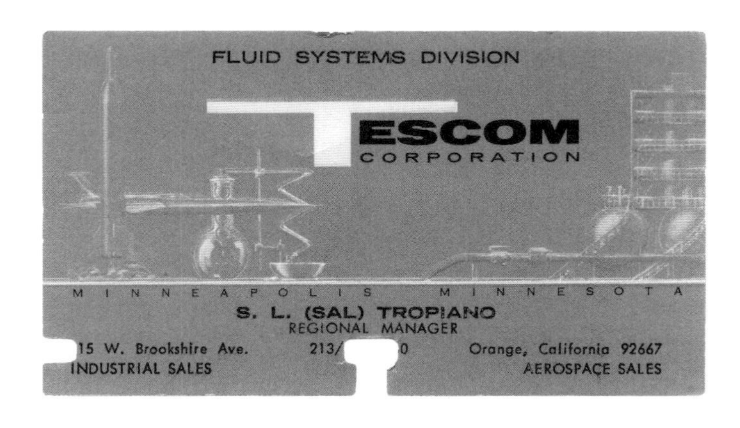
FLUID SYSTEMS DIVISION
TESCOM
CORPORATION
MINNEAPOLIS MINNESOTA
S. L. (SAL) TROPIANO
REGIONAL MANAGER
15 W. Brookshire Ave.
213/
Orange, California 92667
INDUSTRIAL SALES
AEROSPACE SALES

Leading Producer of Plasma Equipment

CHARLES C. POTTER

MANAGER
SPECIAL PRODUCTS

Thermal Dynamics CO DIAL (802) 295-7541

LEBANON, NEW HAMPSHIRE 766

2401 SO. PULLMAN ST.

SANTA ANA, CALIFORNIA
(714) 540-3530

LEROY I. PEASE
CHIEF ENGINEER

HIGH VOLTAGE COMPONENTS
& EQUIPMENT

JESSE STITZER
CHIEF ENGINEER

17 S. LEXINGTON AVE.
WHITE PLAINS, N Y
WH 9-3888

BUS. PHONE 542-1867

RES. 598-6140

MILTON A. RAMPY

PRESIDENT

Utility Trailer Southwest Sales

1601 E. 4TH AVENUE

EL PA[illegible] EXAS

ROBERT V. SALLQUIST
DISTRICT TECHNICAL MANAGER

P. O. BOX 885 / BELMONT, CALI[illegible] 94002 / TELEPHONE (415) 592-2121

VISUAL SEARCH MICROFILM FILE

VSMF

A. C. HOWERTON
District Manager

INFORMATION HANDLING SERVICES, INC.
DENVER TECHNOLOGICAL CENTER ENGLEWOOD, COLORADO 80110
(303) 708

westronics inc.

3605 McCart St. Fort Worth, Texas 76110 817-926-2621

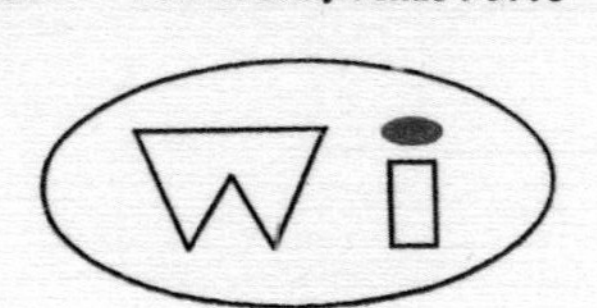

TED MAYER
DISTRICT MANAGER

430 - 40th STREET
OAKLAND, CALIFORNIA
415-653-7909

See Fashion Seal Uniforms

INDUSTRIAL APPAREL

WORKLON

DIVISION OF SUPERIOR SURGICAL MFG. CO., INC.

63 NEW YORK AVENUE, HUNTINGTON, N. Y. 11743

6816 DART STREET
DALLAS, TEXAS
(214) 747-5960

W. A. TAIT
SALES REPRESENTATIVE

1969

BREW

vacuum furnaces

MILTON W. WATTS
Sales Engineer

RICHARD D. BREW and COMPANY, INCORPORATED
AIRPORT ROAD, CONCORD, N. H. 03301 U. S. A.
3 225-6605

Ray Rachkowski

Phone (505) 268-0928 / 209 [illegible]blo, SE / Albuquerque, N. M.

AREA CODE 201/869-7300
DELL OPTICS co., inc.
9226 KENNEDY BLVD • NORTH BERGEN, N. J. 07047
KARL FEUER

(213) 674-2241

CHARLES D. ULDRICKS

DISTRICT MANAGER

HYDRA-SET DIVISION

INTERNATIONAL AIRPORT · 6901 IN[illegible]L HIGHWAY · LOS ANGELES 90045

Delta Data Systems Corporation

H. Barry Maser

Vice-President Marketing

Woodhaven Industrial Park, Cornw[illegible] Heights, Pa. 19020 • (215) 639-9400

AREA CODE 201
835-1300
EXT. 328

H. L. SCHAAF
TECHNICAL REPRESENTATIVE

CHEMICAL PRODUCTS SALES DIVISION
EXPLOSIVES DEPARTMENT
E. I. DU PONT DE NEMOURS & COMPANY
INCORPORATED
POMPTON LAKES, N. J. 074

214—351-3221

Walter E. Shea
Government Markets Coordinator

Eastman Kodak Company
6300 Cedar Springs Road
Dallas, Texas 75235

Kodak

Fred R. Spears
Technical Sales Representative
Mapping and Photogrammetry

Eastman Kodak Company
6300 Cedar Springs Road
Dallas, Texas 75235

Kodak

EXPLOSIVE TECHNOLOGY

A SUBSIDIARY OF DUCOMMUN INCORPORATED

JOHN E. DRAKE

ASSISTANT PRODUCT MANAGER
PRODUCTS DIVISION

P. O BOX KK
FAIRFIELD, CALIFORNIA 945

TELEPHONE
707-422-1880

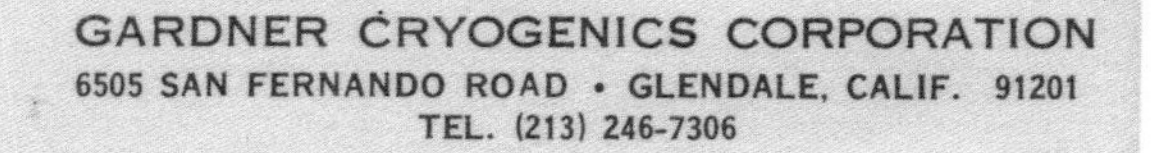
GARDNER CRYOGENICS CORPORATION
6505 SAN FERNANDO ROAD • GLENDALE, CALIF. 91201
TEL. (213) 246-7306

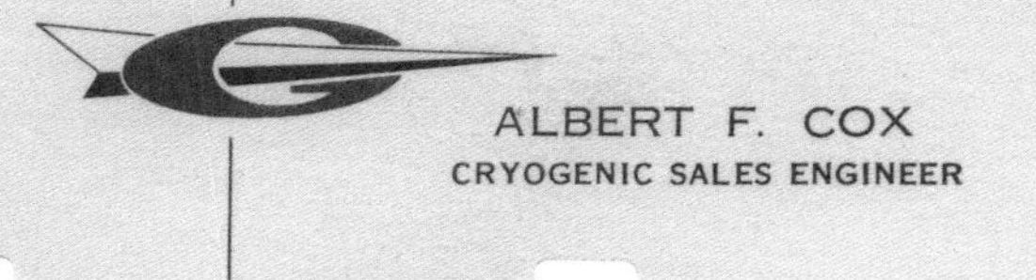
ALBERT F. COX
CRYOGENIC SALES ENGINEER

BERYLLIUM

GENERAL ASTROMETALS CORPORATION

A SUBSIDIARY OF THE ANACONDA COMPANY

LEONARD SMILEY
VICE PRES.
DIR. OF MARKETING

320 YONKERS AVENUE
YONKERS, N. Y. 10701
914 YO 8-2211

Harper Shapes Metals That Shape The Future

H. M. HARPER COMPANY

Morton Grove, Illinois 60053

Fred Fankell

1719 Boulder Avenue
Denver, Colorado 80211
(A.C. 303) 433-7397

TEL.: 721-8300
AREA CODE 216

F. MORGAN COX

CERTIFIED HEALTH PHYSICIST

PRODUCT MANAGER
THERMOLUMINESCENCE DOSIMETRY
CRYSTAL-SOLID STATE DEPT.
THE HARSHAW CHEMICAL CO.
DIVISION OF KEWANEE OIL

1945 E. 97TH STREET
CLEVELAND, OHIO 44106

heat technology laboratory, inc.

4308 GOVERNORS DR. / HUNTSVILLE, ALA.

D. LARRY JONES
PRESIDENT

205-837-2000

World's Largest Produc of Multichannel Analyzers

LAMINEX INDUSTRIES, INC.

Phone: (216) 391-6446
CABLE CODE: IDENTIFY

J. DAVID STONE, JR.

6100 BELLAIRE BLVD. #414
HOUSTON, TEXAS 77036
Phone: (713) 621-0032

5122 ST. CLAIR AVENU CLEVELAND, OHIO 44103

los alamos
scientific laboratory
OF THE UNIVERSITY OF CALIFORNIA
LOS ALAMOS, NEW MEXICO 87544

ROYCE W. JENNINGS
Procurement

P. O. Box 990
Phone (505) 667-4419

LEROY E. WILSON, PH.D

SENIOR ENGINEER

MECHANICS RESEARCH INC.

ALBUQUERQUE DIVISION

1200 UNIVERSITY BLVD., N.E.

ALBUQUERQUE, NEW MEXICO 87106

) 243-5546

Nuclear Measurements Corporation
2460 NORTH ARLINGTON AVENUE
INDIANAPOLIS, INDIANA 46218
PHONE: 546-2415

LARRY G. VAUGHN
GENERAL SALES MANAGER

* INSTRUMENTATION [illegible] HE NUCLEAR SCIENCES *

100 MIDLAND ROAD, OAK RIDGE, TENNESSEE 37830
AREA CODE (615) 483-8451 • TWX 810-572-1078

WOLFGANG REIPRICH
Applications Engineer

AN EG&G COMPANY

E. F. MACKEY
MANAGER
SPACE INSTRUMENTS SECTION

Packard Bell
Space & Systems Division

RANCHO CONEJO INDUSTRIAL PARK
LAWRENCE & ARNOLD DRIVE
NEWBURY PARK, CALIFO

(Area Code 805)
498-3621

plasmadyne

a division of *GEOTEL, INC*

ERICH MUEHLBERGER
MANAGER, HYPERTHERMAL TEST FACILITY

3839 South Main Street, Santa Ana, Calif 92702 •(714) 545-7171 (213) 626-1456

RONALD A. FISCHER
SALES ENGINEER
MICROELECTRONICS DIVISION

5301 CENTRAL AVE., N. E., SUITE 1400
ALBUQUERQUE, N. M. 87108
(505) 268-3549

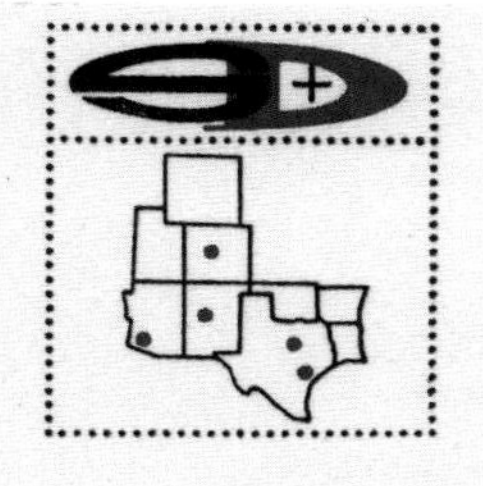

Rick Goodman

SCIENTIFIC DEVICES—*Southwest*

Office: 4300 Silver, S. E., Suite B Albuquerque, N. M. 87108

(505 729

In El Paso and Las Cruces Dia erator, Ask for Enterprise 0172

COMMUNICATION EQUIPMENT

Tel. (505) 268-5300
124 Quincy N.E.
Albuquerque, N.M. 87108

BEN STOLTZMAN

303-442-3837

TRANSFORMER-ELECTRONICS
COMPANY

DEAN C. BAILEY
DIRECTOR OF
RESEARCH AND DEVELOPMENT

P. O. BOX 910
BOULDER INDUSTRIAL PARK
BOULDER, COLORADO 80302

"DEDTRU"
Grinding Fixtures

"TRU-FLUTE"
Helical Grinding
Fixture

UNISON CORPORATION

Ultra Precise Centerless Grinding Equipment

JACK MACKAY
PHONE (313) 544-9500

1143 E. 10 MILE ROAD
MADISON HGTS., MICH. 48067

B. L. "PAT" PATRICK

SALES REPRESENTATIVE

CHEMICAL PRODUCTS

U.S. BORAX

UNITED STATES BORAX & CHEMICAL CORPORATION

)42 S. LAMAR ST. • LITTLETON, (80120 • PHONE (303) 794-5969

AREA CODE 213
983-0763

vacuum / atmospheres corporation

atmosphere specialists

H. H. HERRING

7356 GREENBUSH AVENUE
HOLLYWOOD, CALIF. 91605

(213) 849-6003
843-2730

BOB LIFSEY

VERADYNE CORP.

ENGINEERING SERVICES MECHANICAL PRODUCTS
PRECISION MANUFACTURING

330 NO. VICTORY BLVD. URBANK, CALIF. 91502

Paul K. Yee
Engineer
Sales/Applications

1000 Chalomar Road, Concord, California 94520
Phone (   ) ·6-6660

DRY GLASS BEAD PEENING & CLEANING

CABINETS — BLAST ROOMS — AUTOMATED

Lloyd L. Fortna Co.

DISTRIBUTOR

LLOYD L. FORTNA
PHONE (303) 935-3182

3025 S. HOOKER CIRCLE
DENVER, COLORADO 80219

1970

BEEHIVE
ELECTROTECH
INC.

B.E.I.

1473 SOUTH 6TH WEST
SALT LAKE CITY, UTAH 84104
PHONE (801) 487-0741

DUKE DEFOREST
DIRECTOR OF MARKETING

Technical Services and Special Consultants in
Digital & Analog Systems

BGR² INC

4316 MESA GRANDE. S.E.
ALBUQUERQUE. N. M. 87108
PHONE (505) 268-7959

ROY E. MARCHANT
SYSTEMS ENGINEER

ALLAN S. ABBOTT
CONTRACTING OFFICER

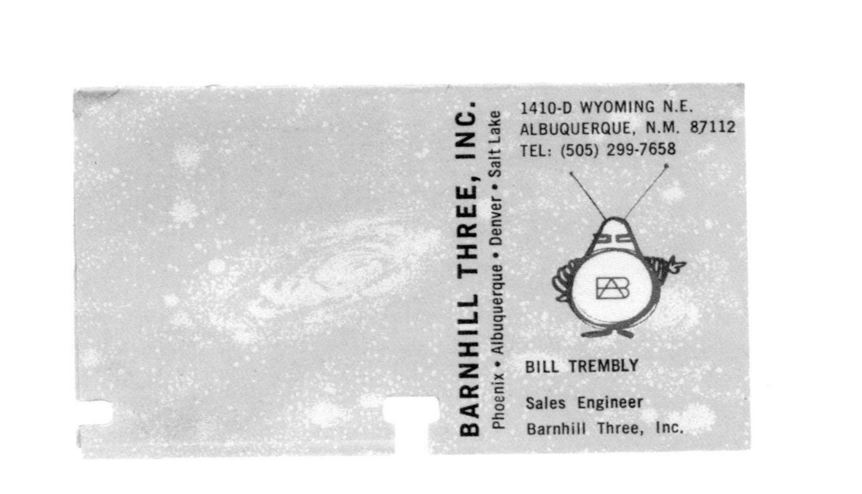
BARNHILL THREE, INC.
Phoenix • Albuquerque • Denver • Salt Lake
1410-D WYOMING N.E.
ALBUQUERQUE, N.M. 87112
TEL: (505) 299-7658
BILL TREMBLY
Sales Engineer
Barnhill Three, Inc.

GOLIATH OF THE WORK GLOVE FIELD

SOUTHWEST OFFICE & WAREHOUSE
3612 BYERS AVE. - - FORT WORTH, TEXAS 76107

MRS. CORRINE BOND
VICE PRESIDENT

PHONE PE 7-3171

617-275-8212

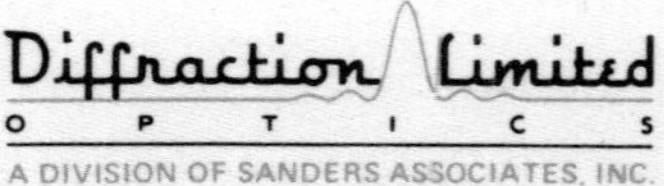

A DIVISION OF SANDERS ASSOCIATES, INC.
Middlesex Turnpike, Bedford, Mass. 01730

CYRIL A. PIPAN
Manager, Technical Sales

DYNALECTRON CORPORATION
AEROSPACE OPERATIONS DIVISION
ALVIN D. HAMILTON, JR.
ENGINEERING MANAGER
PHONE: (817) PE-24481
TWX: 910-893-5003
6000 CAMP BOWIE BLVD.
FORT WORTH, TEXAS 76116

KEN RIDDLE

electronic memories

First Bank & Trust Bldg., Suite 540

Richardson, Texas 75080, Tel. (214) 231-7207

Field Emission Corporation

Melrose Ave. at Linke St. / McMinnville, Oregon / 97128

Richard P. Espejo

M[illegible]er, Field Service Engineering

(503) 472-5101

MICHAEL SCHERMER

MANAGER, ALBUQUERQUE BRANCH

GENERAL ELECTRIC COMPANY

5301 CENTRAL AVE. NE, SUITE 1205

ALBUQUERQUE, NEW MEXICO

(505) 265-3494

(214) 358-1131

WALTER T. McKAY, JR.
SALES MANAGER

GEOSCIENCE NUCLEAR
A Division of Geoscience Instrumer oration
2335A WHITNEY AVENUE, HAMDEN NN. 06518

GREENWAY INDUSTRIES (505) 242-8457

1105 4TH ST. N.W. P.O. BOX 574 ALBUQUERQUE, NEW MEXICO 87103

"BILL" McKINNEY

EXEC. VICE PRES.

JANITOR, REST ROOM SUPPLIES AND EQUIPMENT
ADVANCE FLOOR & RUG MAINTENANCE EQUIPMENT

1401 12TH ST., N.W.   ALBUQUERQUE   P. O. BOX 1735

New Mexico's Oldest and Largest

WALTER MORK   PHONE 247-9555

Explosive Cartridges

Cartridge Actuated Devices

ARTIE SONNIKSEN

TECHNICAL
SERVICES

HOLLISTER, CALIFORNIA

PH. 40 7-5851/TWX: 910 590-0457

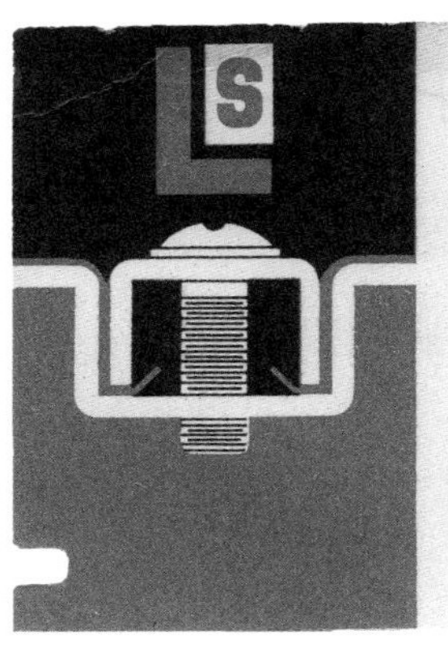

ROBERT ALLDREDGE
Alldredge and McCabe
1550 South Pearl Street
Denver, Colorado 80210
Area Code 303 744-6351

LINDSAY STRUCTURE DIVISION
International Steel Company
1321 Edgar St. • Evansville, Ind. 47707
(812) 425-3311

ROBERT C. DITRICH

FIELD ENGINEER

LORD MANUFACTURING COMPANY
DIVISION OF LORD CORPORA

509 EXPRESSWAY TOWER
6116 N. CENTRAL EXPRESSWAY
DALLAS, TEXAS 75206
214-363-0265

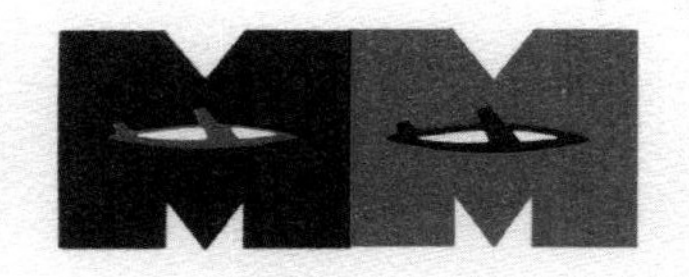

MAGNA MILL PRODUCTS

JOHN A. BROHAMER
sales engineer

1500 SPACE PARK DRIVE SANTA CLARA, CALIF. 95050
PH.: 408 246-9225 246-9222

WAYNE PEACOCK
Sales Manager

(602) 274-3332 [illegible]

Rosemount Partitions

RAY SANDERSON & Associates

MANUFACTURERS' REPRESENTATIVE
FOR THE ROCKY MOUNTAIN STATES AREA
NOPA
REQUEST ANY CATALOGS & P/L

SEND US YOUR ORDERS FOR PROMPT ATTENTION

RAY SANDERSON PHOENIX, ARIZONA 85016
P.O. B[illegible]0434

industrial wiping materials by SCOTT

JOHN H. D. GOEMANS

DISTRICT MANAGER

SCOTT PAPER COMPANY - 1243 [illegible])RD STREET, DENVER, CO 80206

(303) [illegible]-1232

(213) 694-1511

R. W. CRISMON
Western Regional Sales Manager

TEL. 201 688-4600

Unique Wire Weaving Co., Inc.

SPECIALISTS ON EXTRA-FINE WIRE CLOTH

HOWARD H. BEYER
PRESIDENT

762 RAMSEY AVENUE
HILLSIDE, N. J. 07205

Dick Mangold

Engineer-in-Charge

Xerox Data Systems

Fountain Professional Building
9004 Menaul Boulevard, N. E.
Albuquerque, New Mexico 87112
[illegible] 298-7683

1971

James E. Croker
Government Accounts Manager
Computer Products

BASF SYSTEMS INC

7735 Old Georgetown Road
Bethesda, Maryland 20014
Tele. 301-652-4214

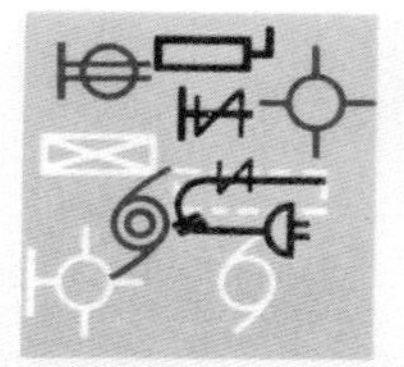

CONTRACTING
AND MAINTENANCE

BoMur Electric Company

INCORPORATED (N.S.L.)

TELEPHONE 247-1044
110 LOMAS BLVD., N.E.
ALBUQUERQUE, NEW MEXICO

DICK SALTER
ELECTRONICS DIVISION

Walter E. Freudiger
District Manager

DATA
PATHING
INC.

5316 W. IMPERIAL HIGHWAY
LOS ANGELES, CALIFORNIA 90045
T[illegible] IONE (213) 649-2833

DIGITAL COMPUTER CONTROLS INC

NUMBER ONE FIRST STREET, LOS ALTOS, CALIFORNIA 94022
415 — 941-0630

KEN LARSEN / WESTERN REGIONAL MANAGER

ELECTROFUSION
CORPORATION

JERRY COLLIGAN
SALES MANAGER

104 Constitution Drive
Menlo Park, Ca. 94025
(415) 324-0074

A. B. WATERS
TECHNICAL MANAGER

HALLIBURTON COMPANY DUNCAN, OKLAHOMA

DICK THIBODEAU
FIELD SALES

HILLEARY
ASSOCIATES

ELECTRONIC MANUFACTURERS REPRESENTATIVE

1811 CARLISLE N.E. · ALBUQUERQUE, N.M. 87110 · 505-265-7631

L. M. "CORKEY" DIAL

HY-TEST SAFETY SHOES • Division INTERNATIONAL SHOE CO.

4842 S. Darlington TULSA, OKLA. 74135

Phone: 918 - [illegible]757

982-4682

OFFICE INCORPORATED

DICK CHAPMAN

441 CERRILLOS RD.
SANTA FE, N. MEX. 87501

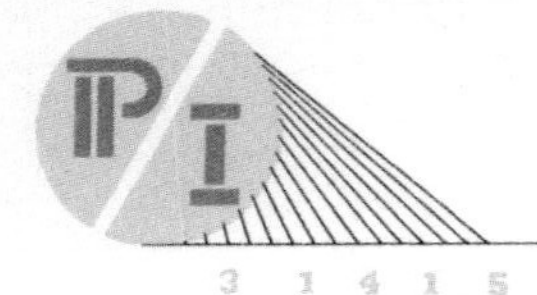

PHYSICS
INTERNATIONAL
COMPANY

3 1 4 1 5 9 2 6 5 3 5 8 9 7

2700 MERCED STREET, SAN LEANDRO, CALIFORNIA 94577

DOUGLAS M. MUMMA
MANAGER, EXPLOSIVE
PRODUCTS DEPARTMENT

PHONE 357-4610
AREA CODE 415

CUSTOM PLASTIC
INJECTION MOLDERS

PUSH BUTTON CONTAINER CORPORATION

P. O. BOX 8768 – 6319 COCHITI S.E. – ALBUQUERQUE, N. M.

DAVID C. FAERBER

(505) 255-7543

TRANSFORMER COMPANY

16625 NORWALK BLVD. • CERRITOS • CALIFORNIA 90701

A. J. (TONY) TIMKO

Dist. Sales Manager **213/926-3361**

JACK DERMODY
Field Engineer

Tektronix, Inc.
Calculator Products

6801 So. Yosemite St.
Englewood, Colorado 80110
Phone: 303—771-8012

A. P. VARNEY

WESTERN CONSTRUCTION SALES

1972

DEADY CHEMICAL COMPANY

OLIN CORPORATION, CHEMICALS GROUP

WATER TREATMENT FOR INDUSTRY

JOE COOPER
ENGINEER
SALES - SERVICE

712 CENTRAL AVENUE, S. E.
ALBUQUERQUE, N. M. 87107
PHONE: 242-3023 (A. C. 505)

ELASTIC
STOP NUT
DIVISION

Union, N. J. 07083

DUANE R. COREY
District Manager

First Bank & Trust Bldg.
Suite 200
Richardson, Texas 75080
214 - 231-2391

ENGINEERED EQUIPMENT, INC.

J. POOL WEBB

(915) 533-4221

BOX 12629 - 4120 RIO BRAVO

EL PASO, TEXAS - 799

e^2i

FUNCTION MODULES, INC.
2441 CAMPUS DRIVE,
IRVINE, CALIF. 92664
PHONE (714) 833-8314

RAY MEYER
Sales Manager

INSTRUMENTATION AMPLIFIERS • NONLIN[illegible]CTION MODULES • CONVERTER MODULES

GREENRAY INDUSTRIES, INC.

840 WEST CHURCH ROAD, MECHANICSBURG, PA. 17055
(717) 766-0223

Greenray Division

ROBERT R. ZEIGLER
R. F. ENGINEERING MANAGER

GROWTH INDUSTRIES, INC.

SPACE AGE MACHINING

CHARLIE ABBOTT
763-7676
A C 816

12515 THIRD STREET
GRANDVIEW, MO. 64030
P. O. BOX 287

ROBERT Q. BUSS
President

Malvern Industrial Park, Malvern, Pa. 19355
Phone: 215-644-7600

R. L. "DICK" PETCHER
AREA MANAGER

JOY MANUFACTURING CO.

4985 COLORADO BOULEVARD
DENVER, COLO. 80216
(303) 388-5891

P. O. BOX 11542, STA. E • ALBUQUERQUE, N. M. 87112
PHONE: ( ) 296-4569

Tel. 315-797-4449

Director of Research & Development

Dr. W. M. Doyle

FIVE WEST WHITESBORO STREET • YORKVILLE, NEW YORK 13495

TELEPHONE (505) 865-7990

Los Lunas

Machine and Tool Co.

ROBERT F. SMITH
OWNER

P. O. BOX 88
LOS LUNAS. N. M. 87031

GTE SYLVANIA

WESTERN GOLD & PLATINUM COMPANY

Wesgo

BELMONT, CALIFORNIA

PRECIOUS METALS • CERAMICS

HARRY MASON
VICE PRESIDENT MARKETIN

525 HARBOR BLVD.
BELMONT, CALIF. 94002
Phone (415) 593-3121

SPECIALISTS IN THE GENERATION OF LIGHT

C. RICHARD PANICO

SALES ENGINEER

39 Commercial Street   Mec   Mass. 02155   617 395-7634

1973

Buehler Ltd.

APPARATUS FOR METALLURGY / GEOLOGY

2120 GREENWOOD ST. / EVANSTON, ILLINOIS, U.S.A. 60204

RAY MICHELS
WESTERN REGIONAL MANAGER

P. O. BOX 57
NORTHRIDGE, CALIF. 91324
PHONE (213) 349-5119

FERROFLUIDICS CORPORATION

DR. RONALD MOSKOWITZ
PRESIDENT

144 MIDDLESEX TURNPIKE · BURLINGT[illegible] [illegible]ASSACHUSETTS 01803 · (617) 272-5206

ROBERT SUBER

1717 SIXTH STREET, NW
ALBUQUERQUE, N. M. 87107

TELEPHONE (505) 243-5656

INDUSTRIAL M ALS DIVISION

BURTON L. SIROTA

WESTERN DISTRICT SALES MANAGER

SUITE 205
2172 DUPONT DRIVE
NEWPORT BEACH, CALIF. 92660
(714) 833-1470

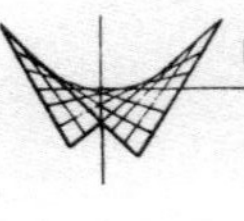

UNIVERSAL PROPULSION CO.

BOX 546 - RIVERSIDE, CALIF., ZIP 92502

FRANK MARION

AREA CODE [illegible] PHONE 685-5966

NORTHWEST WIRE

REP FOR

VECTOR CABLE COMPANY

MARSH MARINE CONNECTORS

MANUFACTURERS OF GEOPHYSICAL, UNDERWATER AND
INSTRUMENTATION CABLE AND CONNECTORS

WILLIAM A. BENNETT (503) 223-3858

4250 S.W. GREENLEAF TLAND, ORE. 97221

Calculators / Computers

Byorklind

DAVE BJORKLUND

WANG LABORATORIES, INC.

1805 SAN PEDRO, N.E.

-BUQUERQUE, NEW MEXICO 87110

(505) 265-5608

WESTERN BEARINGS INC.

Bearing & Power Transmission Specialists

247-0222
24 HOUR SERVICE

CHET REDMAN

1613 FIRST NW
ALBUQUERQUE, N.M.

1974

DELAVAL

GEMS
SENSORS DIVISION

FARMINGTON
CONNECTICUT 06032
PHONE 203 677-1311

ROBERT C. SHOREY

SALES ENGINEER

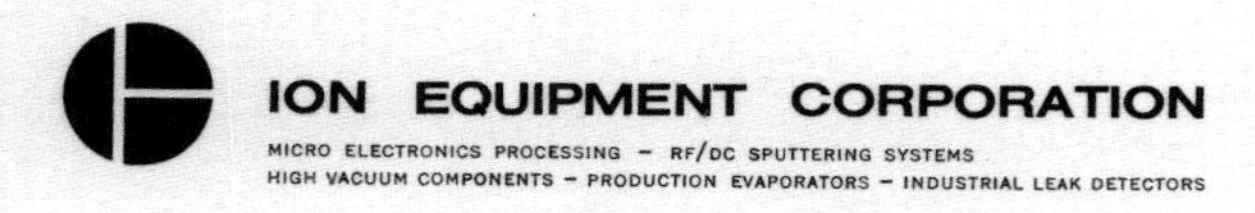

CHARLES M. GRITMAN

PRODUCT MANAGER

1805 Walsh Avenue • Santa Clara, California 95050 • 408-249-4121

Tele. 377

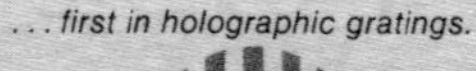

J-Y OPTICAL SYSTEMS

Div. of J and Y Diffraction Gratings Inc.

Gilbert S. Hayat, Ph.D.

Vice President

20 Highland Avenue, Metuchen, New Je[illegible] 08840 ● Telex: 84 4516 ● (201) 494-8660

Magna Tek Systems Inc.
E. L. Oster
President
25393 Huntwood
~~23850 CLAWITER ROAD~~
HAYWARD, CALIF. 94545
(415) 785-0100

A Ainsworth BSc
Radiation Sources Department

The Radiochemical Centre

Amersham England HP7 9L[illegible] [illegible]el Little Chalfont (STD code 024 04) 4444

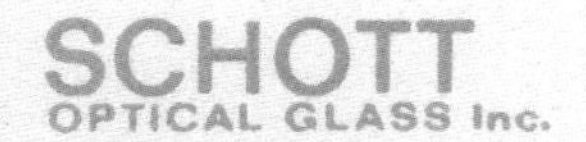

DURYEA, PENNSYLVANIA 18642
(717) 457-7485
P. O. BOX 4111
FULLERTON, CALIFORNIA 92634
(714) 993-1600

ROBERT N. CHAMBERLAIN
ESTERN REGIONAL SALES

1975

TWX 910-950-1180
602-945-2665

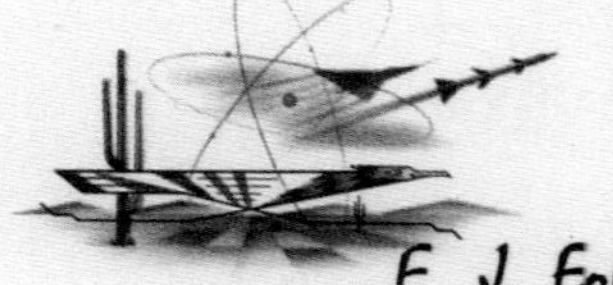

E. J. Foley and Associates

4241 WINFIELD SCOTT PLAZA • SCOTTSDALE, ARIZONA 85251

MANUFACTURERS' REPRESENTATIVE

George R. Tallent
Home: 602 - 947 - 9086

inrad

JOHN B. PALMER
Eastern Regional Sales Manager

INTERACTIVE RADIATION, INC.
406 Paulding Avenue
Northvale, New Jersey 07647
(201) 767-1910

P.O. BOX 1088
BORGER, TEXAS 79007
PANHANDLE
BORGER
COMPLETE STEEL SERVICE
PIPE & STEEL
INC
ROY H. NICHOLS
SALES MANAGER
OFFICE (806) 274-2291
HOME (806) 274-2388

RAY BERRETH
SALES REPRESENTATIVE
CRYOGENIC EQUIPMENT DEPARTMENT

UNION CARBIDE CORPORATION
LINDE DIVISION
100 OCEAN GATE LONG BEACH, CALIF. 90802
TELEPHONE: (21 5-3721

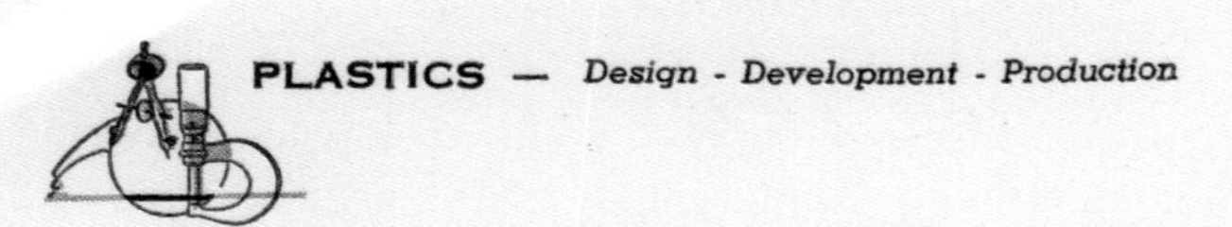

VAN SICKLE PLASTICS CO.

TEL. (402) 432-6944

621 PEACH STREET
LINCOLN, NEBRASKA 68501

STEPHEN W. VAN SICKLE

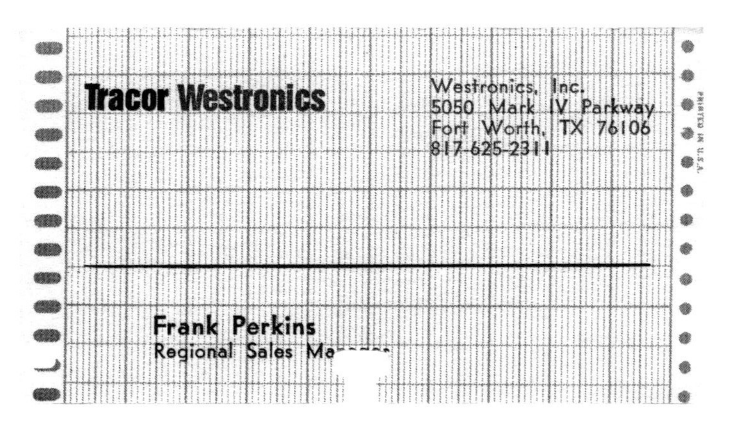
Tracor Westronics
Westronics, Inc.
5050 Mark IV Parkway
Fort Worth, TX 76106
817-625-2311
Frank Perkins
Regional Sales Ma
PRINTED IN U.S.A.

1976

CHUCK R. VOGEL

VACUUM COATING EQUIPMENT

1115 E. ARQUES AVENUE, SUNNYVALE, CALIFORNIA 94086
PHONE (408) 245-9270

ROBERT W. SMID

PHYSICIST

LASER SPECIALIST
DISA ELECTRONICS
DIV. OF DISAMATICS, INC.

779 SUSQUEHANNA AVE.
FRANKLIN LAKES, N. J. 07417
(201) 891-9460

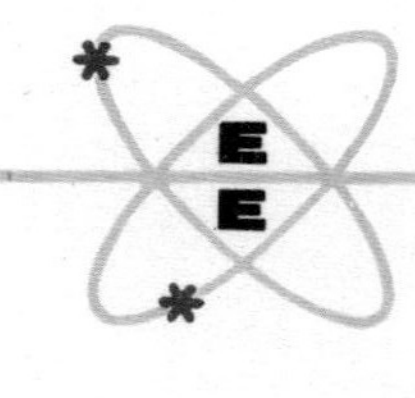

Electronic

Enterprises

I n c o r p o r a t e d

418 Louisiana, S.E. Suite 8
Albuquerque, New Mexico 87108
Telephone (505) 265-2202

Dan Smith

✱ Electronic Manu[illegible]rers' Representatives

POST OFFICE BOX 2688
LEHIGH VALLEY, PA. 18001
215 264-8611

everson electric company

HARRY W. RILEY, JR.
Sales Engineer

Home Phone (201) 454-6631

(612) 941-3300

Dayton Johnson OR APPLICATIONS ENGINEER

PHONE (303) 789-2548

CONTROLS DIVISION
ROCKET COMPONENTS COMPANY
(FLUID & GAS CONTROL EQUIPMENT)

PAUL LOCKLIN

P. O. BOX 1175
ENGLEWOOD, COLO. 80110

1977

Martin Grossman
Technical Representative

32nd & Griffin Ave. Richmond, California 94804
Phone: (415) 234-4130 Telex: 335-358
Los Angeles answering vice (213) 681-6981

P. O. Box 5134 Redwood City, Calif. 94063
Hank Bogardus
Reg. Sales Mgr.
415-365-0800
DAGE
mti
TELEVISION
The Camera People
219-872-5514
DAGE-MTI, INC. 208 Wab
., Michigan City, Ind. 46360

DOUGLAS J. JAMES
SENIOR PHYSICIST

PHONE: 613-592-1460

LUMONICS RESEARCH LIMITED
105 SCHNEIDER RD., KANA[illegible] ONTARIO, CANADA K2K 1Y3

MIKE DEL CASTELLO
Vice-President

Manufacturers of

ULTRA HIGH VACUUM
Flanges — Fittings & Components

285 LAWRENCE AVE., SO. SAN FRANCISCO, CA. 94080
415/87[illegible]2, EXT. 12

NUCLEAR DATA INC.
Golf and Meacham Roads
Schaumburg, Illinois 60196
Phone 312 - 884-3621

ROBERT M. BRUNK
SALES ENGINEER

13287 EAST AMHERST AVENUE
DENVER, COLORADO 80232
OFFICE: (303) 423-4543
HOME: (303) 755-6607

THE PERKIN-ELMER CORPORATION

ANTHONY J. D'AMICO
ATOMIC ABSORPTION PRODUCT SPECIALIST

INSTRUMENT MARKETING DIVISION
15042-A PARKWAY LOOP
TUSTIN, CALIFORNIA 92680
(714) 544-6272 (800) 432-71

ED MORTBERG

(505) 266-7861

(505) 266-7862

SCIENTIFIC SALES ASSOCIATES

130 Louisiana N.E. • Albuquerque, New Mexico 87108

home - 265-5215

ROLAND E IHDE
LIGHTING SPECIALIST

VERD-A-RAY CORPORATION

8013A MARQUETTE N.E. [illegible]BUQUERQUE, N.M. 87108
PHON[illegible] [illegible]8-4755

1978

ED STONE
LIGHTING SPECIALIST

ESC

ELECTRIC SUPPLY
COMPANY, INC.

PHONE (505) 345 [illegible] / 3400 CANDELARIA RD. N.E.
POST OFFICE BOX 1087 / A[illegible]UERQUE, NEW MEXICO 87103

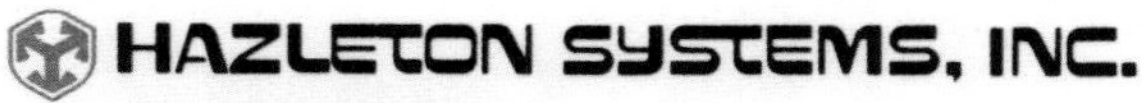

5242 CROOKSHANK ROAD
CINCINNATI, OHIO 45238
TELEPHONE 513-922-4300
TOLL FREE 800-543-7372

MICHAEL J. FARKAS
Laboratory Animal Technologist

First Bank & Trust Bldg #333
Richardson, Texas 75080
214-238-0619

SILENT GLOW/HOEL IRSCHNER/HARDCO/
DYNAC/BIOCLEAN/P AIR/ACME/HARFORD

BILL ROGERS

JOHN WOODSMALL

INTERACTIVE COMPUTERS

THE MICROCOMPUTER STORE

MONDAY THRU FRIDAY: 10 A.M.–8 P.M.
SATURDAYS: 10 A.M.–6 P.M.

217 WEST SAN FRANCISCO
A FE, NEW MEXICO 87501

(505) 982-9997

nuclear shielding services inc

1237 south director st

seattle, washington 98108

(206) 763-0526

- radiation shielding windows refurbished
- consulting
- engineering
- fabrication
- installation
- maintenance
- stud welding
- emergency services

Larry L. Carpenter Sr.

President

LONNIE BOULWARE

WOMACK MACHINE SUPPLY

Distributors of Fluid Power Equipment

2031 Candelaria N.E. • Albuq N.M. 87110 • (505) 345-2511

Your Personal Archives, Inc.

MICROFILMING SERVICES

MICHAEL JOHN P. MCSWEENEY

COUNTRY CLUB GARDENS
SPACE 310
SANTA FE, NEW MEXICO 87501
PHONE 505-471-5662

Introduction by Matthew Coolidge
Edited and designed by Laura Lindgren
Card collection managed by Aurora Tang

The Center for Land Use Interpretation would like to thank Laura Lindgren and Ken Swezey, publishers of Blast Books, and Barbara Grothus at the Black Hole.

This project is supported in part by a grant from the Elizabeth Firestone Graham Foundation.

The Center for Land Use Interpretation is a nonprofit organization dedicated to the increase and diffusion of knowledge about how the nation's lands are apportioned, utilized, and perceived.

The Center for Land Use Interpretation
MAIN OFFICE:
9331 Venice Blvd.
Culver City, CA 90232
www.clui.org

Library of Congress Control Number: 2015031592

ISBN: 978-0-922233-45-8

Published by Blast Books, Inc.
P.O. Box 51, Cooper Station
New York, NY 10276-0051
www.blastbooks.com

Printed and bound in China

First Edition 2016